ESPRESSO VOL. 1

To Jon,

ORLANDO KIMBER

PREFACE

"Truth is the beginning of every good to man." Plato

We need the certainty and clarity of facts and good ethics. **espresso** seeks to invigorate and enlighten you with clear, concise, evidence-based insights about ourselves, our culture, work, society and politics.

I hope the result, like a good cup of coffee, will refresh, invigorate and restore you.

Orlando Kimber, January 2021

SELF

NOUS

W e use the word 'intelligence' to describe the apprehending of relevant facts and the relationships between them. This is vital to good decision-making, as conclusions made from false premises will result in bad choices.

The Greek philosopher Anaxagoras first brought philosophy to Athens in the fourth century BC. He proposed that the mind had the innate ability to perceive the correct order of things and thus to understand what's true or real. This is the origin of the word nous, which is close to our idea of 'common sense' and the feeling of an instinctive recognition for what's good.

In actual life it's almost impossible to have access to all the relevant information, and even then we have to sort it appropriately. It's noticeable that successful entrepreneurs maintain a keen sense of the goals of their organization and the information they need. They are fully responsible for the outcome of their decisions, ask the right questions and are unlikely to be distracted by unnecessary data. They don't use big firms of consultants.

In his 1983 book 'Frames of Mind', the eminent psychologist Howard Gardner offered seven types of intelligence: spatial, musical, physical, visual, verbal, mathematical, interpersonal. Not that we have equal strengths in any of these, but that our ways of processing information are as diverse as the world is various.

Wherever kind of intelligence dominates, the best outcome must be to reach what is true, and we can only feel this in our hearts and gut.

As Heraclitus put it, "Much learning does not teach nous."

LETTING GO

Peak performance in all occupations relies on three key factors: awareness of an intention, all of one's energy available in the present, and total immersion in the activity. Perhaps the simplest example of this is a 100 metre foot race between world-class athletes, whose job is to run in a straight line as fast as possible. Once the race has begun, there can be no strategy and no tactics, just a sprint to the finish line and total self-belief. But as the cockney builder Peter Carrington once told me, 'just' is the most expensive word in the English language, as in "...just another window over there..."

To have total absorption is less about 'doing something' and more about 'being there'. The challenge is one of concentration. We may have physical, intellectual or emotional distractions, so the key is to recognize that each of those faculties is our own responsibility. With training, we can develop the power to concentrate, despite pain, mental chatter, expectations, and distress over real or imagined fears.

There are two strategies one can use here. The first is to be so energized and excited by the goal that it burns away any distraction, but this is hard to maintain over a long period. The other is to allow ourselves to sense the feelings, acknowledge them and let them go. That way we have a chance of living in our greatest self, and thus experience real freedom in every moment.

M.E

O therwise known as Chronic Fatigue Syndrome (amongst many other names), doctors diagnose M.E. after ruling out other diseases. As yet, there is no known 'signature' detectable in blood analysis, and the symptoms are as diverse as those of 'flu. In all cases there is exhaustion and mental fatigue unrelated to exertion. The intensity of the illness - and doctors have confirmed it as a 'real' sickness - can confine the sufferer to bed for months or years. Yet its cause is unknown.

In the West, we appear to have first recognized 'neurasthenia' in 1869, as an exhaustion of the central nervous system's energy reserves. The American Medical Association attributed to the wearing affect of an increasingly competitive and frantic urban society, and popular columnists gave it the nickname 'Americanitis'. Sufferers were normally upper class or professional, and sedentary. It particularly afflicted women. Inevitably, Sigmund Freud attributed the distress to a lack of sexual satisfaction.

Perhaps traditional Chinese medicine would attribute this state to a depletion of chi - that universal energy that courses through a healthy body - resulting in reduced functioning of the five vital organs of heart, liver, spleen, lungs and kidneys.

Although there are both psychological and physiological symptoms, the remedy may be primarily physical. Whilst there is no panacea that works for all, there is time-proven treatment by rest, positive emotions and correct nourishment. If the patient can make progressive physical effort - no matter how small - recovery will eventually come.

KNACKS FOR INSOMNIACS

W hilst the full purpose of sleep remains unclear, we definitely feel worse if we don't get enough. If this sorry state persists, it will affect our health unless we take remedial measures. There's plenty of advice available, such as exercise, exposure to sunlight, and avoiding alcohol by day. There is also abundant guidance on winding down before bedtime, getting comfortable, the right room temperature (less than 21 degrees centigrade) and minimizing noise. If none of this works, it may be an idea to find another way to get your ZZZ's, and this is where the US Air Force may come in useful.

Research done on behalf of flying teams has shown that healthy humans can survive well on four hours sleep and that you can achieve this through naps of between 45 minutes and two hours. Astronauts, who may have difficulty achieving a full eight hours sleep when in space, use an anchor snooze of four hours and a nap of two and a half.

The knack for insomniacs is to find a way to a regime that suits our individual body rhythms, our daily schedule, and gets the full benefit of both the deep and rapid eye movement (REM) phases of sleep.

Monks who habitually do heavy physical work, report that they need less sleep when in retreat and more when labouring. The great violinist Yehudi Menuhin kept a punishing routine into old age and attributed his naps of fifteen minutes after lunch - with complete silence and solitude - as critically important.

If you need rest, you must grab forty winks.

INHIBITED BY LIGHT

Melatonin is a hormone that occurs naturally in animals, plants and microbes. In herbs such as Feverfew and St. Johns Wort, it regulates the response to light and works as an antioxidant in defence against harsh environments.

A hormone is a messenger chemical. Melatonin, released from the pineal gland, interacts with the human immune system and signals daylight-dependent activities, such as social behaviour and skin colouring. A melatonin boost results in increased drowsiness, and because a certain frequency of blue light inhibits its production, this can interfere with our sleep / wake mechanism.

Experiments have shown that exposure to 39 minutes of low level incandescent light can halved our melatonin response. In the modern world, this is the norm, whereas in ancient times our ancestors would spend the evening in the amber glow of fire-light to prompt the release of the hormone. In clinical trials, small amounts of natural melatonin yield early onset of sleep whilst high dosage leads to a dramatic increase in vivid dreams.

Although some people swear by the efficacy of synthetic melatonin to help with jet lag, scientific studies show little evidence of benefit to those suffering insomnia, disruption from shift work, or sleep disorders from drug abuse.

Research continues on the proposed health benefits associated with the use of melatonin and Europe now allows it on prescription, whereas in the US it's available as a 'food supplement'.

CRAVING

The Republic of South Africa sentenced Nelson Mandela to life imprisonment in 1964. He spent the next 18 years on Robben Island and the everyday concerns that bother most of us - such as wealth and influence - were not issues that preyed on his mind. Instead, he focussed on improving personal qualities entirely under his own control; such as honesty, sincerity and generosity.

This discernment is a skillful way of dealing with a circumstance that one would otherwise regard as negative. He learned to create contentment by developing resources he could enjoy in the present. He continued to work toward different a condition, but wholly accepted the current situation.

Despite the brutality of Robben Island, Mandela

freed himself from unhealthy cravings which would therefore lead him both to the removal of disappointment, and to a peaceful state of mind.

The key to this is to know what will and what won't bring us sustainable happiness. Thai Buddhists refer to this ability as a 'coolness', to distinguish it from 'thirst' of desires or anxiety.

Scientists have also studied the response to craving impulses in the brain. Using MRI, they've identified that alcohol, drug and food addictions all relate to the same three areas of the brain that serve memory, perception, emotion and learning. In theory, if a sufferer exercised these areas of the brain, they could reduce the compelling power of stimulants. The addiction would lessen.

Scientific experiment has now shown that distraction helps to stave off cravings, and the longer one persists, the weaker the urge becomes.

FASTING

When people talk about losing weight, they mean they want to lose fat. The only way to do this is to use up more calories than you take in, which means we need to eat less and exercise more.

Fasting is a cure that beasts of all sorts have used since Creation and doctors rediscovered it in the health movements of the early twentieth century. Digestion is the most energy-consuming function of the body and therefore when any animal fasts, this energy becomes available to improve the body's condition. Just as a finger heals after a cut, our body spontaneously seeks to repair itself internally if given the opportunity to do so. This fasting instinct is usually obscure to those of us with a typical Western diet, which features high levels of stimulants such as sugar.

All spiritual traditions worldwide - including Hindu, Muslim, Christian and Buddhist - recommend fasting for the development of patience, humility and clarity of mind. Perhaps the health benefits were just as obvious to those who founded the festivals of Lent, Ramadan and others.

Fasting is not appropriate for those with eating disorders such as bulimia. The traditional Ayurvedic medicine of India emphasizes that the process should be gradual, gentle and beneficial to both the body and mind.

Whether you fast for spiritual, physical or for protest reasons, if done wisely and to a moderate degree, the benefits include increased self-confidence, energy and weight loss.

NO NEED TO SUFFER

Dentists apply local anaesthetics for the control of pain and inflammation, and to moderate the nausea and anxiety of patients. Locals work by blocking the signal along the nerve path to the brain, whereas a general anaesthetic stops the brain itself from recognizing signals. Negative response to a general, though rare, is very serious and can cause death. Therefore, the British Dental Association asserts that dentists should only use general anaesthesia in extreme clinical cases if they have thoroughly investigated all other methods. They also assert that a skilled anaesthetist should administer a narcotic, with immediate access to hospital care if required.

Adverse reactions to a local are rare and typically

occur because of unskilled use. At the time of writing, Lidocaine (aka xylocaine) is the favoured chemical for locals because it comes on quickly and lasts for one and a half to two hours. It's often combined with another drug to reduce the speed at which it's absorbed into the bloodstream, thus sustaining the effect. A dentist may also use nitrous oxide (laughing gas), which gives the patient a welcome feeling of being distant from the situation and even euphoria. There are also combinations of chemicals which repress recall of the procedure in the patient's memory.

Dentist have successfully used acupuncture and electrical stimulation (TENS) to interrupt nerve signals in pain management. Hypnotherapy may be especially useful for those who feel fear before treatment, as it's proven to reduce anxiety, pain and the need for post-operative drugs.

CELEBRATION OF THE INFINITE IN THE FINITE

Our birth endows us each with certain inner resources including degrees of health, strength, and intelligence. Our place of birth and parents will bring out qualities of character, relationships and opportunities which we may or may not cultivate through education and training. How we exploit these to our own benefit is a measure of our material success in life. If you create and sustain a remarkable company employing thousands of happy employees, then the results are publicly clear and measurable. We may regard the degree to which we benefit others as a spiritual success. If one's role is to care well for an elderly relative who requires constant attention and support, then that achievement may pass unrecognized in society but be equally powerful.

How then gauge one's justifiable satisfaction with life in public? There is, of course, no need. The only person who needs to feel content is oneself. In terms of personal fulfilment, society's opinion is irrelevant. It may make us happy to receive praise, like the sun cutting through dark clouds on a rainy day, but it doesn't have any value in itself. Money is a medium for exchange, whereas we measure wealth in the capacity to enjoy life.

The final arbiter will undoubtedly be ourselves when, at the end of life, we slip back into infinity. Then we will know the degree to which we've been able to celebrate the mystery of our being within this finite world.

CULTURE

LADY GODIVA

The eleventh century legend of Lady Godiva arose from the historical figure of Countess Godgifu (literally 'God's gift'), an Anglo Saxon noble married to Leofric, one of the four earls of Britain appointed by Cnut the Great of Denmark. Godiva was a devout Catholic and worshipped the Virgin Mary, to whom many of Europe's greatest cathedrals were dedicated. That much seems certain. From this point we may or may not proceed from legend to myth...

In 1016, Prince Canute (his coronation was later in the year) and the Danish Army destroyed Coventry and the nunnery there. The people of the town, just 69 dwellings and not the city it is today, were suffering so badly that Godiva begged Leofric to reduce the taxes on them. Her pleas fell on deaf ears until he eventually agreed to accede on one condition: that his wife should ride naked through the town. When one considers that in the eleventh century, it was disgrace enough for the public to see a noblewoman without her jewellery, this would have been unthinkable. Such was Godiva's compassion (or fury at her husband), that she agreed to the contract. Accounts vary from this point on, but the one that's gained most popularity is that Leofric commanded the townspeople to remain indoors as the Countess rode through the market, veiled only by her long blonde hair. Just one person broke the covenant, spied on her through a hole in his shutters, and was struck blind for his transgression.

Hence the term 'peeping Tom'.

BOOTS THE BISHOP

Albertus Magnus was a 13th century philosopher and theologian, working as a Dominican monk in the Catholic church. His early education included instruction in Aristotle's writings and he subsequently undertook to study and comment on these, as well as translations made by the Arabic scholars ibn Seena (aka Avicenna) and ibn Rushd (aka Averroes). In doing so he became central to academic debate, and ultimately in shaping our view of ethics today. He was a prodigious author in science and philosophy and studied through literature, direct observation and experiment. Like his contemporary Roger Bacon and Albertus's own pupil Thomas Aquinas, he was a master of both systematic method and comprehensive description. A large amount of his own scientific knowledge was accurate and useful. His collected writings on botany, mineralogy, astronomy and many other topics come to 38 volumes in all.

He became a bishop, and during the three years in this role his reputation for humility grew. As he refused to travel by horse and instead walked back and forth across his huge diocese, he became affectionately known as 'boots the bishop' by his parishioners. In semi-retirement, Albertus became renowned as a mediator, which was perhaps essential in his advocacy. He asserted coexistence of both science and religion and the importance of knowledge and reason in both.

The Church made Albertus a saint in 1622. He is one of only 34 Doctors of the Church, referring to those who have made a special contribution to doctrine or theology.

IN PRAISE OF GREATNESS

On a night-time visit to Durham Cathedral, there was no doubt that we were in the presence of greatness. The atmosphere was rich with candlelight and a mantra-like chant; rising, falling and resonating across the vast hull of the nave. Entrancing as it was, the source of the inspiration was the building itself.

As one entered by the great cathedral door with its ancient sanctuary ring, the power of place was overwhelming. Although illumination came solely from tiny bulbs and candles, it was enough to sense the vast pillars soaring upward to the vaulted ceiling. They're like enormous trunks of ancient rainforest trees that draw the eye to a canopy far above in the distant gloom.

There were hundreds of other people in the building, and I'm sure they all felt the swelling of the heart that accompanies such an emotion. Everywhere one looked - and we confirmed this by a return to visit the cloisters and garden the next day - there was symmetry, proportion and mystery. It is living proof that architects can avoid flaws through the perfect co-operation of many people in realizing a grand vision, designing with immaculate care, working artfully with the materials and constructing with supreme understanding and skill.

A human being has to learn all of this by themselves as they build their character. However, whether it's a building or a human, when we're in the presence of true greatness, we cannot deny this quality.

●

SAMUEL JOHNSON

The man of English letters, a poet, essayist, sermon writer, critic, biographer and creator of the most commonly used English dictionary for over 170 years, was born in 1709. He suffered poor health, poor eyesight and severe depression. From reports of his nervous tics, face-twisting and blowing noises, it seems likely he also had Tourette syndrome.

He didn't receive his degree from Oxford until 27 years after he'd started it. Money problems interrupted his education and financial difficulties plagued much of his life.

At the age of 37, a group of booksellers commissioned Johnson to compile a comprehensive dictionary. The task was to last nine years (though planned for three), and required the help of six full-time clerks, to copy the numerous quotations and definitions he used to illustrate the 42,773 entries. It was neither the first or a unique publication, but it proved to be very popular.

Tragically, his wife died before he completed the work, and he suffered an anguish of guilt, perhaps quickening his faith as a devoted Anglican. He took in and cared for sickening friends, surrounded himself with company (perhaps to stave off the dreaded 'black dog' as he called the depression), and actively promoted women intellectuals. His home and workplace at 17 Gough Square in London - rented when he began work on the dictionary - stands today as an authentic reminder of his spirit. The ambience there is as hospitable as the one who overcame serious handicaps, to become truly great.

AN UN-INFORMATION SOCIETY

As a schoolboy, a teacher described meditation as something he wouldn't try, as it sounded too much like hard work. As someone who had learnt to meditate at the age of 16 and found it to be beneficial, this confused me. He was trying to be witty, but showed that he was ignorant. It confirmed what I already knew, that this wasn't a teacher that I wanted.

When the UK announced a series of library closures threatening up to 20 percent of the system, it seemed equally unreal. It's exactly at this time of challenging employment markets and the need for everyone to develop new and better skills, that both kids in school and adults need access to further education and the riches of reading. If you don't have a computer or access to newspapers, how will you keep in touch with the world and the job market as it unfolds? If you don't have room to store books at home, where will you find and read them? If you can't afford expensive reference works, how will you get access to them? Meanwhile, South Korea, a country that encourages ambition on steroids, has allocated the equivalent of £300m to open up 180 libraries.

The world may be in dire straits, but let's not extinguish the sparks of interest in learning at the very moment that we should fan them into flames of enterprise and enlightenment. Otherwise we'll look back at this as a time of a comprehensive destruction of opportunity and the bonfire of our hopes.

◉

FLUENCY

There are certain qualities that inspire others to follow one's words and these include clarity of diction, logic, directness, a sense of spontaneity, enthusiasm and emphasis. Public speakers have the advantage of non-verbal cues such as presence, eye contact, and a sense of communing with the audience. A writer must get a message across in black and white without these aids.

Mahatma Gandhi was infamous as a poor public speaker early in his career, because his voice was weak and his physical appearance was unimpressive. Yet he came to influence millions both in his lifetime and afterward, through the power of his authority and conviction, based on personal experience and integrity. Delivery then is only half the art. There must also be something to say and for the speaker to prepare it carefully.

Toward the end of his life and during the decline of Athens in the fourth century BC, the Greeks considered Demosthenes as their greatest orator. They revered him alongside Homer. Like Gandhi, Demosthenes developed a robust constitution through exercise and further cultivated his mind through memorizing great classical works. These informed the construction of his famous speeches. Despite his powers of persuasion, foresight and judgement, a declining Athenian empire ignored his warnings. They had lost their sense of public virtue and energy and failed to gain their independence as a state.

The ultimate irony was that Demosthenes took his own life, rather than die at the hands of a former tragic actor - Archias - who led the forces pursuing him.

◉

FUN

In the 1680s, the word 'fun' meant to cheat or hoax, but 50 years later the sense had transformed into entertainment or amusement. The spirit of the original verb carries through to today in 'to make fun of', and perhaps this gives the clue as to the change of meaning.

No doubt Neanderthal man poked fun at one another for the size of their tools, but historians attribute the origins of satire as an instrument of social and political comment to Aristophanes in Ancient Greece. This had a formal link to comedy as opposed to tragedy.

By the ninth century, the Arab author Al-Jahiz used satire to leaven a treatise on a serious subject with something more amusing. When writing on zoology, he quipped: "If the length of the penis were a sign of honor, then the mule would belong to the honorable tribe of Quraysh."

Political life and royalty are ready subjects for a jibe, so when Elizabeth I's subjects used satire freely and fruitily to express their disillusionment, it was subject to censorship from the end of the 1500s. This increased under Puritan influence.

The Age of Enlightenment dawned in the late seventeenth century and the next hundred years saw a renaissance of pungent satire in books and plays to ridicule both individuals and institutions. Perhaps it was on this tide that fun became synonymous with entertainment, and later bore Dickens, The Simpsons and Pussy Riots in its wake?

I SING THE BODY ELECTRIC

At Walt Whitman's death, the press reported that over a thousand mourners visited his coffin within the first three hours. During his life, the frank expressions of love for the human body in his poetry - particularly in the collection Leaves of Grass - caused outrage amongst some, not least for its frank and ambivalent sexuality.

The self-publication of Leaves of Grass moved Ralph Waldo Emerson to send a five-page letter praising the work. It's clear that Whitman, Emerson and their contemporary Henry David Thoreau, all shared similar humanist sentiments, and a reverence for the individual's capacity for the transcendental. All three were philosophers but were not just theorists. They wanted to relate their thoughts to everyday lives.

What marks out the poem 'I Sing the Body Electric' is that it uses both the nuts and bolts of the physical frame and life in a human being. It digs for something essential that we can't see, but only feel. It's as if Whitman is praising the body as a perfect miracle - the more so for being commonplace - and saying to us, "Look at this amazing creation; this is proof of greatness."

The poem is in free verse, for which Whitman is famous (though not the father of the form) and this unfettered scattering of words must have seemed particularly liberal when it was first published.

The great gift of the poem - and of Whitman, Emerson and Thoreau - is that within them ran the deep vein of faith that, to be alive, is itself the greatest blessing.

ECSTASY

The root of the word ecstasy is the Greek ekstasis meaning 'standing outside oneself'. Its modern use is solely to describe an euphoric feeling or rapture, accompanied by a sense of time-lessness and goodwill. Because of the association with a state of mind beyond the ordinary, religions have a general agreement on the beneficial nature of such peak experiences, though the importance attached to them differs.

The drug MDMA (street name 'ecstasy') can allegedly directly post the user into just such a blissful state, although the effect wears off and has a corresponding 'down'.

The Buddhist Pali Canon notes eight levels of trance in meditation, leading to what's termed 'total absorption'. These self-induced experiences expand the ability of the practitioner and have no unpleasant side-effects.

Balinese kris dancers are a spectacular example of a trance-induced ecstatic state. In the authentic experience, the subjects undergo a personal sense of transformation. They demonstrate other-worldly powers by pressing gimlet-pointed kris knives at their sternum as they writhe to the incessant rhythmic, flowing musical accompaniment. Less dramatic, but equally absorbing, followers of Sufi - a branch of Islam - attain ecstatic states through concentration, breath and their graceful spinning motion.Their devotional act is inspiring to both the performer and the viewer.

Whether we achieve states of bliss through sex, devotion, sport, dance, music, stimulants or rituals, the result leads to a way of being that allows us to feel more joyful, reassured, loving, hopeful and connected to others.

●

WORK

FLASH CRASH OF 2:45

Algorithms are now responsible for over 70% of the trading on the US stock market; mathematical formulae that talk to one another to optimize financial transactions. Two thousand physicists work on Wall Street to support this Black Box trading aka algo-trading or high frequency trading (HFT). Yet in 2010, something happened that no-one could control. In just five minutes, 9% of the value of the stock market 'disappeared' in what's known as the flash crash of 2:45. Algorithms are so dominant, that the only thing that will overrule their interactions is a big red button marked 'Stop'.

The formulae run on computers, which process information fast. As they dominate the market, this also moves faster than lightning. The digital round trip of the 827 mile fibre optic line from New York to Chicago used to take 13.2 milliseconds (ms). That's five times faster than the click of a mouse. A lightning bolt would take about 18 seconds. In 2009 a new fibre-optic line shaved 0.3ms off the journey. This is useful if a fund is seeking to arbitrage the price between a futures contract in Chicago and an asset in New York.

Algorithms are everywhere, not just on the stock market. Amazon auctioned an out-of-print book called 'The Making of a Fly' at $1.7m; its 'value' rose to $23.6m without a single purchase thanks to electronic trading. Decision-making algorithms are here to stay, and we need to develop alongside them. Fast.

◉

OBJECTIVE ANALYSIS

The 'scientific method' uses reason to uncover relevant facts and associations, and let reality speak for itself. The motive behind this is to engage in an enquiry on the true state of something, by studying the elements of it without personal bias or opinions. It therefore follows that anyone else could investigate the same phenomenon using their own set of tests and measurements, and come to a similar conclusion, as long as their method was sound.

Before embarking on a voyage into the unknown, it's necessary to have a goal such as a sound decision, proposition or hypothesis. Without a central purpose, it's impossible to test the data. As one accumulates information, it's also necessary to verify facts by seeking second parties who can confirm the findings, or by probing at information with a healthy dose of doubt or scepticism. This will, to delve and scour, shows the rigour of the analysis. Inaccuracies creep in if we skip this stage.

Inevitably, there's a point at which the volume (or lack) of facts becomes bewildering. It is then that one needs to classify the key elements into some kind of organizational tree; with the trunk as the core challenge and the branches as the principal areas of concern. After the intellectual grunt work, it's down to imagination and creative thinking to review and understand the interconnections. Without this crucial step, you're left in a sterile sea of statistics with no insight, meaning, or life.

●

WAS HENRY FORD A QUANTUM MECHANIC?

An affirmation is a statement in which one makes a positive assertion to oneself or others. Confirmation is subtly different, because it's a statement made to establish reality. Some hypnotists use affirmations along with visualizations to condition the mind and generate a state of well-being, confidence and mindfulness. Recent scientific experimentation in quantum mechanics has some interesting results pertaining to this.

Rutherford Appleton Laboratory, near Oxford, England, enables the study of material at sub-atomic levels. They've confirmed that some particles exist only when they're observed. When they're not obscrved, they don't exist. Because many such particles make up our physical world, a logical deduction is that when we put our attention on an outcome, we create those very circumstances.

Steve Jobs seems to have had the habit of practising this, in what became known to his colleagues as the 'reality distortion field'. Whilst some could accuse him of wilfully rewriting history despite the obvious facts, many celebrated him for harnessing this force to achieve remarkable results. Jobs was so powerful in his application, that teams accepted the 'impossible' as a real possibility. The results are there for all to see.

Back in 1931 Henry Ford used the same unwavering determination to get the V8 engine developed in a single casting at an affordable price, when experts agreed it was impossible. Perhaps this gave rise to his most famous quote: "Whether you think you can, or you think you can't, you're right."

THOUGHT EXPERIMENTS

E instein's reputation as a mathematician and physicist is the stuff of legend, however his aptitude for abstract thought is less well documented. Perhaps his love of music and reverence for the third century BC mathematician Euclid were early signs of this extraordinary mind, which could meld both creative imagination and logic to a sublime degree. He was also a great communicator and whilst travelling, would write daily to his wife Elsa and to his adopted stepdaughters. On his death, he left over 3,500 pages of private correspondence.

One way that Einstein synthesized the two sides of his brain was by thought experiments designed to reveal a truth, through a method that starts with known facts and builds a case through additional information. For this to be successful it also helps to have skill as a storyteller, because by appealing to our emotions, the elements become vivid and thus memorable.

Thought experiments are not exclusive to the sciences and are evident in the philosophical work of Plato (predating Euclid by a century) who used dialogues between characters to illustrate his points. They're also a familiar tool for the lawyer's arguments in court. The paradox of The Buttered Cat playfully illustrates this, as it's based on two axioms. When dropped, a cat naturally lands on its feet and hot buttered toast traditionally lands the wrong way up, so what happens when we attach toast to a cat?

As Einstein said, "We cannot solve problems at the same level of awareness that created them."

PLATO'S PARABLE

"Imagine there was a Prime Minister with a bigger social media following than any of his other party members but is slightly deaf, shortsighted, and limited in statesmanship. The Cabinet argues with one other about strategy, each thinking they ought to be the boss. None have learned the art of leadership, but all insist that no-one can teach this and are ready to punish anyone who disagrees.

Naturally, they do all they can to persuade the PM to give them the helm. They form into cliques, but they know that if one group gains dominance, their rivals will gossip to the press about past indiscretions; incapacitate the Prime Minister; take control of the Government; help themselves and their friends to improper expenses and turn the democratic process into a drunken free-for-all. Ultimately, they have to give way to the person who can best manipulate the man or woman at the top. They achieve this by praising the PM's knowledge of 'the people' and condemning everyone else as worthless.

None of them understand the true politician. If a statesman is to be fit for the job, they must study the economy, the environment, the differing communities, new and old policies and all the other aspects of managing a country and its people. Others think it's impossible to gain the professional skill needed for such control (not that they can conceive of it) and that there's really no such thing as an art of statesmanship. In such ignorance, won't the Members of Parliament regard a true leader, should they meet them, as a spin doctor and schemer and therefore of no use to them at all?"

AN IMITATION of Plato's 'Ship of Fools' allegory (from The Republic)

BEHIND CLOSED DOORS

A survey by Paolo Pinotti, working for the Bank of Italy in 2012, researched the effect of organized crime on Apulia and Basilicata during the 1970s. These neighbouring regions showed a sudden slowdown of economic development, and an equally alarming increase of murders compared with other areas of the country. The report concluded "the advent of organised crime coincides with a sudden slowdown of economic development."

The financial crash of 2008 caused a massive loss of both trust and confidence in business, and with the finance industry in particular. Since those dark days, the scrutiny of commerce has increased; regulators now require companies to declare details of corporate ownership, holdings, payments, tax obligations and much more. What could possibly go wrong?

Large organizations who are subject to public scrutiny, also seek to be unaccountable as 'mistakes' attract censure. For this reason they conduct critical meetings "behind closed doors", claiming that they would lose precious competitive advantage or intellectual property. They know that they're behaving with less than perfect transparency, and both the staff and the public recognize this conduct as corrupt. These stakeholders are the very people who need to have trust in shared values, and the confidence that the organization will conform to social standards.

The result of opaque governance is to undermine communication, weaken performance and create unease. The cruel truth is that those who are bent on running their business outside the law will continue to do so, if the rewards are high and the risk of being caught is low.

●

DESDEMONA

The first black protagonist in Western literature is Shakespeare's Othello, 'the Moor'. When his military career takes him to Cyprus, he elopes with the beautiful daughter of a Venetian senator. His wife is the young, pale-skinned Desdemona whose name literally means 'ill-fated, unfortunate.'

And so it comes to pass.

A young officer, by the name of Iago, convinces the General that his wife is having an illicit relationship with another man. The play then reveals the descent of Othello from a noble in love to an irrational, violent and insanely jealous murderer who strangles his wife.

Iago's motives are not clear, but the themes of

racism, jealousy and betrayal pulse through the work. In public, he is charismatic and friendly. He is skilled at convincing others that he beyond suspicion and a trustworthy counsel. However, the soliloquies reveal his manipulative nature in which he seems driven to destroy his commander Othello, Desdemona and the innocent lieutenant with whom she's accused of adultery.

The moral of the story is clear: that it takes only one person with a destructive nature, albeit hidden behind the veil of service, to wreak havoc. The only insulation against this is for a leader to be so free of emotional instability, that the tale-bearer cannot sway their wise judgement. Whilst it's common for those in command to have self-assurance, how many leaders have the qualities of character both to behave ethically and to weed out disloyalty before it becomes outright treachery?

CONGRUENCE

Whilst integrity is the honest commitment to one's own values, congruence is the general agreement between two parties on a single set of beliefs. Not that every value must be in exact alignment, but enough to allow both sides to work together in the trust that each will honour an agreed code of conduct. When parties have to write the code down, it usually points to a lack of trust between the two sides. However, when both factions are fully engaged in the writing of a contract, it can be a useful way of clarifying the principles of a partnership.

When an organization renders laws or other rules into text, there is the danger of them being taken literally and not in the original spirit of cooperation. As the Tao Te Ching - written over 4000 years ago - says, "The more that a state makes laws and order prominent, the more thieves and robbers there are." If a business relationship breaks down, it's usually clear to all witnesses which party has broken with a covenant. Such is the nature of legal battles, that counsel - a paid accomplice - can twist the very simplest statement, to condemn the innocent and glorify the guilty. As one wise adviser said to me, "people get the solicitor they deserve."

On a happier note, there is a sense of trust and therefore relaxation when one knows that colleagues or lovers are playing by the same rules as you. This breeds great opportunities for creativity and the promise of real satisfaction at work or in the home.

18 SECONDS

Back in 1984, Dr. Howard Breckman - a clinical professor of medicine at the University of Rochester - conducted a study into patient care. He discovered that on average, a doctor interrupted patients just 18 seconds into an explanation of their condition. Less than two percent completed their story. Fifteen years later, a follow-up study showed a marked improvement...to 23 seconds.

Other research reveals that only 15 percent of patients fully understand what their doctor tells them, and half are uncertain how they're subsequently meant to look after themselves.

The core of this is the patient-doctor relationship which, when it works well, is conducive to improvements in health. It may therefore be of help if, before a visit to the surgery, one prepares a clear storyline that details the status quo (how your body works normally), the challenge (the first occurrence of the symptoms), the 'rising action' (the re-occurrence and severity of symptoms) and finally the crisis that led to seeking treatment. Being armed with this script can give one the confidence and determination to present your case.

Perhaps it's also worth considering that the patient-doctor relationship is similar to that between a manager and staff. Those at the coalface are the first to know when something operational is going wrong (and probably have a handle on what needs to happen). If their manager doesn't ask (or won't listen), then how can they agree an accurate diagnosis and remedy?

●

SOCIETY

RECLUSIVITY

Over 700,000 (and perhaps many more) young people in Japan, have had no social contact outside of their homes for the past six months. These are the 'hikkomori', literally 'being confined', who find it so difficult to become integrated in society that they opt-out; often choosing to spend their lives in the parental home.

The first generation of hikkomori are now in their forties and some have spent twenty years in isolation. Whilst the symptoms are easy to recognize, the causes are more obscure; the condition typically starts with school absences and then grows through the early twenties. Growing up 'different' in a strict, conformist society set amongst a world of rapid change, must be especially challenging in a crowded and complex urban environment.

The rigorous and competitive Japanese schooling system, together with the pressure to succeed in a career, has set high expectations. A difficult economy since the early 1990s has seen an end to 'a job for life'. Part-time work can mean insufficient income to start a family.

The unhappy withdrawal of hikkomori distinguishes them from the larger generational movement of Hodo-Hodo zoku (the So-So tribe), who've rebelled against the doctrine of hard work and even passed up on chances of promotion to minimize stress. However, at least one hikkomori has turned his isolation into a benefit by using his time to trade in the stock market. Takashi Kotegawa turned a US $20m profit in just ten minutes, in the unusual case of the Mizuho Securities J-Com incident.

UNIVERSITY

The earliest gatherings of scholars and teachers
were communities dedicated to philosophy
and wisdom. By the eleventh century, universities
regarded the arts of grammar, rhetoric (discussion)
and logic, as the necessary tools for the study of arith-
metic, geometry, music and astronomy. Yet the
university persisted as being more than 'the place
where these four roads meet'. In the twelfth century,
travelling scholars had the right to unhindered
passage in the interests of education. Eight hundred
years on, 904 universities from 88 countries affirmed
this academic mobility by agreeing up to support a
new Magna Carta Universitatum.

The emphasis on modern universities in the UK
is to instruct in skills, promote the power of the mind,

transmit common standards of citizenship and ensure that teaching remains focussed on uncovering truths through respect for research. We value the undoubted social benefit of three or four years at college just as much as the academic ideal; a university is a powerful resource for the student to begin a career and a life. This is when the love for what you do can combine with the highest standards. The resources of a university can provide great cooperation and critical thinking from both colleagues and tutors, and establish a platform for something remarkable.

Although a student may arrive at university with the simple willingness to learn, they are being given the opportunity to create literally anything that their imagination can conceive.

THE OLD SCHOOL TIE

An open society is one that's responsive and tolerant and allows people to make the most of themselves. A closed society is one in which decision-making is opaque, controlled and with a rigid social structure. Which do you live in? If you're reading this, it's likely you're part of the former because you have access to the literature which makes the ideas, cultures and beliefs of a large part of the world available to you.

Nine out of ten British people want a meritocracy (a feature of a successful open society) and yet only two out of ten believe this exists in the UK. With statistics like this it's natural that all political parties agree that it's a 'good thing', but how to attain it? The popular answer is better pre-school education, and metrics that forecast whether prospective university graduates are likely to excel from further education.

In the UK in 2013, 80 percent of judges, 70 percent of finance directors and 50 percent of top journalists were educated at independent schools. is changing, but the accusation remains that the system favours private education. Seven percent of children educated at state schools attain AAB grades in 'A' Level, compared to 23 percent of privately schooled kids. Yet those state school pupils are 50 percent more likely to get a first class degree than their more privileged peers. A good degree generally means a good job, so perhaps social engineering will work. What about those at the very bottom of the academic pile? We need to remember that greatness in life does not rely on school grades.

NEWSPAPER VALUES

In 2012 there were over 234 English-language newspapers in circulation worldwide, ranging from the Buenos Aires Herald to the Pyongyang Times. The Acta Diurna of Ancient Rome were the earliest government announcements carved into metal or stone. Sixteenth century Venice saw the circulation of avvisi, which were public or secret handwritten newsletters distributed as political, military or economic 'warnings'. The UK had to wait until 1702 for its own Daily Courant. The largest circulated English language newspaper in the world (2020) is now the Times of India, who claims 15.2 million readers from a circulation of 2.4 million.

The medium has changed and so has the writing, but 'yellow journalism' has always been around, and continues to rely on sensational news, calculated to anger or otherwise excite the reader. There's been a steady decrease in the circulation numbers of newspapers worldwide since 1999 and revenue continues to slide, particularly from advertising.

Thankfully, a few news providers follow a code of ethics that encourages journalists to take responsibility for the information they provide. This commitment by reporters and publications to research, fact-check, and print relevant articles is being sorely tested. How many places can one routinely find original, informed opinion, thought-leadership and the championing of freedom of expression? These are valuable and unique assets for an open society.

Data may be more plentiful and delivered faster than ever through the web, but good decision-making still relies on accurate and digested information. Reliable and credible editorial teams are a vital resource for citizens of an open society, whether we read the news in print or on a screen.

FREEDOM OF SPEECH

Article 19 of the UN Declaration of Human Rights recognizes "the right to freedom of opinion and expression." This isn't an absolute. It allows us to communicate our opinions and ideas in whatever way we want, as long as it doesn't conflict with other important rights. Transgressions may include defamation, inciting hatred or encouraging overthrow of the established order. Yet even these limitations have limits.

John Stuart Mill wrote in On Liberty in 1859 that, "truth drives out falsity." This is the basis of his argument that we should celebrate free genuine discourse, no matter how odious the opinions of others. It's only when debate is vigorous and wide-spread that it wakes us up from the "deep slumber of decided opinion." He recognized that we need to be fully aware of facts and prejudices, both as individuals and as a community, to perceive truth. He also recognized that what serves as a truth for one era may be inadequate at a later date. Things change.

Mill also recommended that a citizen should be free to express themselves to the point of it becoming a clear and direct threat to another person or group. In our globally connected society, perspectives and values will inevitably come into conflict. Whilst some argue that giving offence is sufficient harm, we're going to have to develop greater tolerance to endure the outpouring of others' bile. Equally, we also need to be precise in defining a threshold, and the consequences for those who go beyond it.

FALLING BACKWARDS

A prison experience will inevitably include gang leaders who have some tactical control of the environment. As fifty percent of convictions are for drug offences, there also will be subcultures and mental problems. When the justice system then releases offenders back into normal life, they have to contend with the same social situation that they left behind, with the possible added challenges of social alienation and stigma from a criminal record. Whilst the external problems for someone living in brutal conditions in society are obvious, the mental and emotional challenges are not.

UK statistics from 2003 disclose that more than half of males and one third of females convicted for a crime, will re-offend and find themselves back in the slammer within three years. Some of these will be psychopaths, the term used for those who feel little empathy or compassion and therefore lack remorse for the harm they do to others. Typically, they derive satisfaction from anti-social behaviour and find it difficult to learn from past mistakes, even when they suffer negative consequences for their actions. Such a distorted view of reality doesn't respond to prison treatment unless the system address the root cause of their condition. Ironically, the prison system is more likely to release psychopaths, who themselves are more likely to relapse. There's even a name for it: recidivism.

The characteristics of a lack of empathy and its flip side, a desire for importance, are not exclusive to prisoners. We easily recognise the same traits in business and other groups, where an individual known for their charm has such a compulsion for personal gain, that they will ignore the resulting harm done to others. Such is the common demand for 'productivity' under current economic conditions, they are likely to continue benefitting until their business cannot make a profit.

●

A CUSTODIAL SENTENCE

F or a legal system to impose a punishment it must have a rationale, whether it be retribution, deterrence, enforcing moral boundaries, removing the criminal from doing more harm, rehabilitation, or making good the damage done to a victim. Any of these may attract a prison sentence and thus a loss of liberty and civil rights. Yet whilst detention may be easy to impose as a punishment, it is not uniform worldwide.

Typically, a judge weighs the evidence in a case and determines a penalty. Custody is the legal, guarded control of a prisoner and is a corporal punishment, although it doesn't mean that the system intends physical harm. However, there are jurisdictions worldwide in which hard labour, poor food, isolation, general discomfort, sleep deprivation, humiliation and denial of visits, are all explicit in the legal system. In South East Asia, for instance, male drug traffickers may typically receive up to 24 wounding cuts with a heavy soaked cane. Beatings are common in many jails worldwide.

Both Plutarch and Quintillian, in Rome during the first century AD, spoke out about the dangers of physical punishment, and stressed that it was impossible to ensure that those in authority did not abuse such measures. Although Tacitus (a contemporary of Plutarch and possibly a pupil of Quintillian) offered a perspective on imprisonment of political dissidents, "If you would know who controls you, see who you may not criticise." Perhaps he was thinking of another comment by him, "the more corrupt the state, the more numerous the laws."

●

HIJACK

In 1996, six Iraqi men forced a landing of a Sudan Airways Airbus at Stansted Airport in the UK. The authorities arrested and jailed the hijackers, only to release them one year later. They based their successful defence on "duress of circumstances" which, they claimed, the courts had not properly heard. One hijacker told the court, "We had no choice but to leave the country in the manner that we did" because they were fleeing Saddam Hussein's regime. There was no retrial and 16 years later, the authorities granted two of the six indefinite leave to remain in Britain.

Seeking political asylum through hijacking an aircraft has precedents, but it raises the obvious concern of the ends justifying the means. Macchiavelli's Il Principe (The Prince) advises rulers that they "ought not to quit good courses if he can help it, but should know how to follow evil courses if he must." In the 1996 case of hijacking for asylum, judges found that indeed, the ends did justify the means, and that the period of confinement was sufficient punishment for the misdeed.

We often see corporate profit or 'shareholder value' put before the interests of people, the environment and wildlife, and some governments freely exploit the fears or gullibility of the public to meet their own objectives. We can see their motives in issues ranging from local council housing developments right up to the second Iraq war. Who then do we call to account or ask to make a judgement?

NDABA

Many successful tribes have used the principle of consensus for government. In Africa they call this Ndaba (aka indaba or indzaba). The aim is to make a decision that meets with common approval. The guidelines are simple, in that everyone may speak their mind and show approval, with no restriction on repetition of ideas, contradictions and dissent. This is an ideal; human nature and the run of conversation will have its way!

However, this is a public process of reasoning and, to function well on matters of importance, it needs everyone to show scrupulous respect for one another. Likewise, the exchange of information needs to be free and allow speakers to express themselves without further obligation, as the forum enables all people to get involved and interact beyond the boundaries of any special interest group to which they may belong. To prevent public disorder, this has to continue outside of the assembly and it's no coincidence that we call this civility - the behaviour proper to citizens; this cooperation is the foundation of civilization.

Such groups need a chairperson who will listen carefully and guide the assembly to consensus without expressing their own opinion. The tribal chief will often play this critically important role, and as Nelson Mandela commented: "When you want to get a herd to move in a certain direction, you stand at the back with a stick. Then a few of the more energetic cattle move to the front and the rest of the cattle follow. You are really guiding them from behind." He paused before saying with a smile, "That is how a leader should do his work."

●

POLITICS

ANEMONE

The sea anemone is a sophisticated killer.

When a small fish or shrimp brushes against the many sensory hairs on its tentacles, it triggers a harpoon-like structure that attaches to the flesh of the prey and injects a dose of poison to paralyze it. The anemone then draws the helpless victim into the digestion system, and that's lunch.

This story will be familiar to fans of Pixar's Finding Nemo as the eponymous hero is a clownfish, a species immune to the sting of the anemone and which can therefore exploit the haven of toxic tentacles as shelter from predators.

Tragically, no such protection was available to Georgi Markov, the Bulgarian writer who was so fiercely critical of the communist regime in his home country, and the victim of the infamous 'umbrella murder' on the streets of London in 1978. Markov was travelling to his job at the BBC, when an assassin used a gun within an umbrella to inject him with a platinum-iridium pellet measuring less than two millimetres in diameter. The toxin ricin, contained within the slug, caused Markov's death from organ failure just a few days later.

The Times newspaper of London reported that the prime suspect for the murder was an Italian named Francesco Giullino (Gullino), who reputedly worked on behalf of the People's Republic of Bulgaria. In 2000, ten years after political reform, Bulgaria posthumously awarded Markov their highest honour for his confrontation of the communist regime. A British documentary in 2006 revealed that Giullino continues to travel freely throughout Europe.

◉

HUMAN RIGHTS IN EUROPE

Whilst we may think of 'human rights' as a modern idea, intellectuals in Europe widely debated the concept in the Age of Enlightenment during the 17th and 18th centuries. The challenge of allowing freedom for an individual within a community goes back to the earliest dawn of humankind.

Since 1950, Europe has enjoyed the Convention of Human Rights, which is the only code that recognises the individual as a participant in international affairs. If the European Court finds that a state or party has violated a person's rights, it will pursue compensation for the victim. However, at the time of writing in September 2020, there's one country within all of Europe that doesn't have a democracy, and is therefore not a member of the Council of Europe: The former Soviet state of Belarus. Although there are concerns about Kazakhstan and Azerbaijan (and the former Soviet Union, Turkmenistan and Uzbekistan outside of Europe), Belarus is the sole state that's maintains the death penalty as statute law. In the former, asylum seekers, anti-government protesters and human rights defenders may encounter harassment, police brutality, torture, and unfair trials resulting in imprisonment. Only in Belarus do 'grave crimes' lead to execution, following a criminal justice system that itself stands accused of avoiding due process. Families of the condemned are not informed, have no chance of a farewell, and are not told of the burial ground.

John Stuart Mill wrote in On Liberty in 1859 that the "tyranny of government needs to be controlled by the liberty of the citizens" and that government should use power "for the prevention of harm." Not killing people.

INTERSTITIAL GUIDANCE

It's known that invasive cancer cells move into healthy tissues along the paths of least resistance. These are the interstices, the spaces between organs and within structures, which channel the progress. The spread of ideas within a social network, both actual and virtual, appears to follow a similar model of behaviour.

Whilst both the physical structure of a networking site and the density of its population are important, so too are the ways people think. If a community is ready for an idea, it's because they accept the basic beliefs and values behind it. A credible agitator may excite interest, but if both the concept and the population are in harmony, the 'Bingo' effect will follow.

Old school advertising based it's choice of a tv channel to reach an audience by the number and type of viewers, and the programmes they watched. Viral ad campaigns go a stage further, and measure the degree to which sales prospects are saturated with ideas or messages. The idea is to trigger a large cascade. This recalls the criteria used by ecologists for assessing the likelihood of dominance by an invasive species of plant. The four conditions that support its success are the ability to grow and reproduce rapidly, to tolerate a variety of conditions, to compete hard for resources, and lack challenge from other species.

Thomas Jefferson had words to say about a government using public money to manipulate social discourse and communication: "...to compel a man to pay taxes for the propagation of opinions which he disbelieves and abhors, is sinful and tyrannical..."

●

YOU CAN'T TAKE IT WITH YOU

The first recorded example of inheritance tax (IHT or 'estate tax') was in the seventh century BC, when the Arab Islamic Empire conquered Ancient Egypt.

Whilst other governments have seen fit to introduce IHT as a utility to raise cash for war, there is also a philosophical basis. Thomas Jefferson, a founding father of the US, a democratic Republican and reader of Adam Smith, said "The earth and the fullness of it belongs to every generation, and the preceding one can have no right to bind it up in posterity." Karl Marx would have said a big 'Amen' to this (had he been religious), as The Communist Manifesto gives high priority to the abolition of inheritance. Jefferson and Marx would have further agreed that great inequality in wealth - the spirit and principle of a genuine republic - hobbles citizenship. Subsequent American presidents Hoover and Roosevelt also marked their disdain for the 'idle rich'. They condemned wealth, not earned by merit, as being "to the great and genuine detriment to the community at large."

A lurch in favour of the richest 15 percent of the world population, has resulted in greater disparities, and the global breakdown of communities requires us all to be more independent economically; we can no longer depend on a network of family or local support, as was the case 100 years ago. Governments worldwide need to make an urgent review of wealth taxes to protect the welfare of ordinary people and make greater efforts to reveal the private funds hidden in tax havens.

●

HIDEAWAYS IN ANGUILLA

The Caribbean island of Anguilla is an Overseas Country and Territory (OCT) of Britain and receives European Aid to encourage economic autonomy. Britain has responsibility for her foreign affairs, defence, internal security, public services and 'the offshore financial sector'. It's attractive for high net worth individuals and businesses to have an Anguillan company as they're anonymous; there is no tax on personal income, capital gains or profit; and corporate compliance is low. It is a 'pure tax haven'.

The taxation regime has come under particular scrutiny. Anguilla has committed to treaties from the Organization for Economic Co-operation and Development (OECD) to share information, making it less desirable for companies avoiding tax to have bank accounts there. The absence of banking facilities doesn't prevent money laundering but makes it harder, because cash can't directly enter the financial system without being detected. However, there are plenty of other nefarious techniques such as trade-based laundering, where invoices are over or under-valued to disguise the movement of money.

Whilst it's laudable for Europe to support Anguilla in the development of a strong independent economy, surely both the European Commission and the UK should examine the ethical nature of that independence? If this is a British territory, then it should have the same ethical standards, legal infrastructure and supervisory practices applied to businesses as those in Britain. If this is true under normal circumstances, then at a time of heightened terrorist activity we need particular scrutiny of hidden assets. When the major trading partners are North America and the Caribbean region, there is surely the need for a close investigation of this. Not to do so would give rise to another kind of OCT; an Official Conspiracy Theory.

●

GAME THEORY IN LAS MALVINAS

I t's believed that there are substantial untapped gas, mineral and oil deposits, in the region around the Falkland Islands. In 2007, Britain prepared a submission to annex further regions of the seabed, "beyond the 200-mile limit but less than 350 miles", according to the Law of the Sea division at the UK Hydrographic Office.

In typical English understatement, they also acknowledged it was "all a bit tricky", because the coast of Argentina is only 300 miles from the islands, which are themselves 8,000 miles from the UK's own shoreline.

When the military junta in Argentina invaded the islands in 1982, oil was at the end of a long bull run at about $32 a barrel. By 1998 it had dropped to just $12 a barrel. In 2012 it was between $89 and $128, making the islands an attractive asset. It's a volatile commodity.

The obstacle for any aggressor - other than the necessity of mobilizing armed forces and the support of the population for an invasion - is the British, who legally own, inhabit and defend the territory. The last war there took 907 lives.

It's reasonable to suppose that Argentina would like to protect its own claims to the seabed within their existing territorial waters, and to have a share in a potential offshore energy harvest. So perhaps Britain and Argentina can devise a joint venture that benefits both parties? One that secures the peace and well-being of the islanders and saves the lives of both the respective armed forces.

MILITARY STRATEGY

The use of war in the name of national interests is common. The role of the military may appear to be obvious, but the grand strategy of politicians, not generals, govern its actions. Armed force is just one of several means to fulfil their aims. Because of this, there's two and half thousand years of written guidance, starting with The Art of War by Sun Tzu, which presents 13 key elements of warfare. The author emphasizes the supreme importance of "attacking the enemy's strategy", in order that political and military leaders may "win first and then go to war." History records that dictators such as Hitler and Stalin had no need of such wisdom - with appalling results - but CIA officers read it with profit.

Whilst leaders may be excellent at finding a

credible 'causus belli' to invoke public support, their skill in warfare seldom goes beyond defining a single strategic goal. For this reason, it's essential that good advisers are available (and listened to) so they think through the strategic options, major scheme, actions and constraints in this, the last resort and the most grave of political actions.

As the Art of War makes clear, the tactics that work in one campaign are unlikely to do so in another due to the change of conditions such as relative fighting power, technology, terrain and disposition of the foe.

Genghis Khan terrorised his enemies and then out-manoeuvred them through superior mobility. Terrorists of the modern era follow a similar strategy through use of the internet and media. When war threatens, one must discover who is pulling the strings.

◉

STERLING CRISIS

In 1973 the Arab led Organization for Petrol Exporting Countries (OPEC) played a gambit that yielded two benefits. By restricting the supply of oil to the West, they prompted a US demand that Israeli troops withdraw from the (Arab) Palestinian-occupied territories. The same oil embargo disrupted the supply chain for fuel and pushed up prices around the world. It established a tension, which to this day remains at the centre of international concerns about energy supply.

At the time of the OPEC action, there was a left wing government in the UK who followed a policy of high public spending. By 1975, inflation ran at over 27 percent and, in an article called 'Goodbye Great Britain', the Wall Street Journal pronounced that the financial market had overvalued sterling. In March 1976 the Bank of England sold sterling and cut interest rates, and by autumn the pound had lost 20 percent of its value. The IMF stepped in at this point with a multibillion-pound loan, together with strict conditions for deep cuts in public expenditure. By 1979 a right-wing government had taken over on a programme of fiscal austerity.

If some of this sounds familiar - overspending by a government, high oil prices, quantitative easing and an austerity programme - then it will come as no surprise that we may face another 'crisis' in sterling. After all, if you were to accept a large cash injection into your business, you'd expect to dilute your share-holding, wouldn't you? It's only odd that no-one's mentioned this...

MORALITY IN POLITICS

The idea of virtue at the heart of all good
decision-making is common to both Aristotle
and Confucius. These two figures established a
philosophy behind rulership, both for the West and
for China, that lasted over two thousand years. Even
Macchiavelli recognized the need for a set of values
by which to govern, it's just that he believed these
differed from personal values.

In Bob Dylan's autobiography, he asserts that
"Morality has nothing to do with politics." Maybe in
some places, at some times, and perhaps right now
but, broadly speaking, that's not the way it's worked
in the past. Whether it's assumed by force, or given
by a mandate from a community, government wields
power. The authority behind this power therefore

exists on a continuum somewhere between the brute selfishness of a small group of people (an oligarchy), or a popular vote which trusts that a leader will make wise decisions on behalf of the tribe, club, state or country (a democracy). In the latter case, one accepts that the rules may not all be to our liking, but believes that they work for the benefit of the entire group to which we belong. In this ideal state the judgement of the leaders discerns what is helpful for citizens and decree laws that protect and nurture the society to which we belong. Morality is at the heart of this system because it centres the ethos on the welfare of one and all.

●

AFTERWORDS

REVIEW / NEWSLETTER

Review: Your opinion of **espresso**, given as a review on Amazon, is highly valuable.

Newsletter: You can get updates on new books, discounts, and other information by signing up at the website.

ABOUT THE AUTHOR

About Orlando

Orlando was born in London, in the UK.

He toured as a classical guitarist in his teens, then worked as a music producer and composer in tv and film.

Orlando went on to advise media technology companies in the early stages of the digital revolution. He played a key role in the launch of the internet in Europe, and the transition to digital production and broadcasting.

He writes non-fiction and fiction, and lives in Cornwall.

Thank you Boo, for your constant inspiration.

espresso is a publication from orlandokimber.com

Cover design by Modern Activity

First e-print: January 2021

Printed in Great Britain
by Amazon

56045088R00063